A FAMILY IS A HOUSE

DUSTIN PEARSON

Poetry

C&R Press
Conscious & Responsible

Cover Art by Rachel Kelli
Interior by Jojo Rita
Copyright ©2019 by Dustin Pearson

ISBN: 978-1-949540-01-7
Library of Congress Catalog Number 2018956128

C&R Press
Conscious & Responsible
www.crpress.org

For special discounted bulk purchases, please contact: C&R Press sales@crpress.org. Contact info@crpress.org to book events, readings and author signings.

A FAMILY IS A HOUSE

for the fathers who left, for the fathers who stayed, and for the fathers who came back

TABLE OF CONTENTS

Pulse

Behind the run of each wall in the house is blood, and in each of
its rooms, one of us, and though the blood bleed slowly, the house
won't heal, and though the house hold no heart, the blood rushes.
To its wounds, we bind ourselves. We ensure it lives in each of us,
in each of us, its pulse. We fill with brisk blood we take into us,
blood thick black in our stomach. Our body swells, and over our
eyes form a bleed that sees only blood. We remain when the house
falls. We move out into the world, thirst true, and in every place we
find bleeding, we eat of a thing that won't do.

II

A Subtext for Violence

Mom and Dad aren't speaking in the next room.
The dark hides both of their torsos, but you can still
see their lower bodies. They're holding hands
even if Mom is crying. A low frost runs over
everyone's feet. Nothing's left to turn the heat on.
In your room, you're left to your own devices,
danger of the outside world impressed on you.
You click on the television to find it. You flip
through the channels, each image a switch
you haven't turned or imagined. Seeing someone die.
Between seven turns on the dial you glimpse your first
and second. A man with a gun in his hands. A face
downturned in mud. Blood running over water over dirt,
it's not enough, not yet. Can you stay innocent now
that you're thinking clever, that you're trying to know
for yourself what you don't yet? Rummage through
the trashcan. Find an empty two-liter. Fill it again
with water. Add a few drops of ink from an old red marker.
Now you have a body filled with blood. Take it outside.
Don't take any of this seriously. Your parents might hear
you stirring. They're occupied. Take your time. Your siblings
are asleep and way behind you. You could explain to them
what in this goes badly. Take a pen, a blunt sub for a knife.
In the body, make punctures. Be excited. Be frightened
when they make a spill in a cold wash down the driveway.

Blood at the Beach

Circumstances make us a car of three
that day. I confuse the crabbing trip
on the muddy dunes for family day
at the beach. The flip-flops I wear
on my feet make my missteps
heavier, each sunken foot harder
to pull up. Even when I've let the Earth
eat both of my shoes, it refuses to give
my balance back, only the support
of the open oyster shells to lodge
where my heel looks to support me
when I fall. I lift my foot quickly,
but the cut is already deep. I don't
look where I feel the pain instantly,
only where the blood trails snakelike
through the mud into the salty sea.
It doesn't take long for the parents
to see. Only one comes running.
While she's still far out, I watch
as blood makes the ocean smoky
and soft. As more goes, the billowy,
creamy cloud it creates storms off,
resigning a small volume of that body
to disposition. Even though it's vitals
of my own body, I continue to watch.
Do nothing. Imagine all of the oceans
murky and blood thick.

The Flame in Mother's Mouth

There's a fire inside our mother's mouth.
Every time she opens it, we throw wood in.
The flames moss
up the sides of her face,

make red-orange pigtails above her head.
No matter how big they get, they won't hang.
She holds on to them while she chases us.

With enough wood, the flames
come out her ears, down her nose.
Our mom is on fire and chasing us,
but doesn't notice. We don't get it.

In our mouths, the wood does nothing.
We keep throwing wood
until the house burns down.
We've lost everything when we tire

and let her catch up to us, wrap us
in her inferno. We roast. The debris floats
to the sky, freezes. Our house returns to us,
pepper ash between flecks of snow.

The ice turns cold on us and we laugh.
We laugh over the glaze of things
that burn us black.

Paternity

The door swung open. It was Dad. He was back after 400 years.
My brothers and I were still dangling, nailed to the wall
where he left us, arms excitedly skyward at the sight of him
like we knew he wanted. He picked us up one by one and tossed us,
swung us through the air at arm's length, letting us hang by our armpits
in his face. His mouth gaped. We reached in, curious
about the smell of the opening, convinced we could take it
in our hands. We searched inside him, and where we saw
after reeling our limbs in, a paste. We smeared it
on our heads, and from every place it touched, hair fell.
We giggled, threw the residue against the wall
and watched it drool the darkest stains. Dad used ties
to bind the hair together, not quite covering the bald patches.
He brought gifts: pacifiers for the lot of us. And those, too,
smelled like him, wherever he'd been. The last time he was here
we had chicken and a blue juice to drink. It was our first day
with big boy cups and out our mouths the juice ran
to the floor below us. He hadn't wiped up, hadn't cleared
the scraps of chicken and gristle before taking off.
The flies that gathered over our mouths and waste thrived,
flying to and running over the heels of our feet, passing along
their gratitude, tickling us through the time before he came. But now
we can finally get down, our two grasping hands we curl to gripped fists
on his lower lip, stretching it to where it lets us touch ground,
but we don't use the lip to run away from him, only wrap it over ourselves.
He's our dad. We finally have a confidence that if he ever left again
he'd have to carry us in his mouth the way we always carry him.

The End of Brother's Tail

Our brother has a tail, and we all play with it.
He'd been on the toilet for days.
Stomachache, he said.

We'd all taken bets.
It would either be green
or yellow-specked with blood.

The tail made its debut out his lower back.
It was mute, a separate issue from the stomachache.
Our brother stayed on the toilet for thirteen more days.

It grew so much
we had to crack the bathroom door
and wrap it around the banister, the stairs,

let it out into the backyard,
and then under the fence
to the front yard.

It changed the routine for those weeks.
There were two bathrooms in the house.
Brother was in Dad's,

so Mom boiled water for his daily use.
I was let in the downstairs bathroom.
My brothers had the woods to use.

Mom would call Dad a dog
each night he came home from work,
which made him mad and talk trash

and take his anger out on all of us.
Under the light in the street,
me and brother Bernie

would jump rope with Brother's tail until Dad
would come out and beat us with it. Meanwhile,
Brother would be tickled.

The faint vibrations of tail against flesh
made ignorant pleasure for him. Mom hated that.
She'd hear our screams, come out, hit Dad,

and at the end we'd all be sitting in a row puffy and slapped.
Brother's tail grew to the need of wrapping it
several times around the house.

You wouldn't believe the consideration we had to give.
The winters were cold. We had to insulate it
to no extreme contrast from the temperature

of wherever Brother was. We'd approximate distances
for family trips, be sure there was enough tail to make it,
adding for the steps we'd take within our destination.

There were the smaller pests, ants, for instance,
and the snack they'd make of whatever section
of the tail was closest. It changed

the way we cut grass. Brother developed
a complicated fear of not being able to see the end of it.
I remember running a line of it through the chimney

to the attic and eventually to a small hole
in our bedroom. He'd dangle it over himself
in small circles until he fell asleep.

We wanted so badly for something to happen to it.
We dreamt of the tail growing so big
we'd have to monitor the time zones,

working for years to buy facilities
to store it in. All our lives
would wilt over the effort of him.

Beat Sounds

When Dad beats us,
we're careful
we don't make sounds.
He'd be fucking us.
The slap of his belt
against our skin
and our sounds
would make
pleasures
for him
like all the women
we've heard about.
In silence,
the belt howls.
It howls
to find nothing
but him again
at the end.

Heroes

Mom can fight. She's my hero.
On the days we wake and find
the walls bloody, we see her
composed and head wrapped,
bacon sizzling beside beat eggs,
bubbling grits. The only of us boys
to miss Dad once we realize
he's gone again is Earl, but only
until the orange juice and sausage,
when he remembers that Dad's mouth
would cut his portions. Us kids
all sit at the table necks up, beaks
open. Mom drops the rations straight
to us. So much the same they are,
Earl and Dad, such curses that cause
each to be the other's favorite
between clashes and absences.
How frustrating to find where
preference betrays investment,
where the former is given and the latter
an effort abandoned. A hero can't be
swept along like trash, even when
they leave, teaching all the ways
love won't bring them back,
and the anything done to deny that.

A Palace of Ice

Mom mostly cries at night. We don't always know why. We could sleep through it, but we stay up with her, as if staying behind a door across the hall might make it fine. We huddle with each other under covers, flashlight beaming or eyes closed pretending to be asleep. Sometimes her crying streams under the crack of our door. Before long it's bed level. The bedframe sinks, but we lift up from it on the mattress. We use our hands to paddle. Everything in the house is ruined and wet, then everything turns dangerous. Us boys make off surviving Mom's sadness. We open the door and it drains. We let our mother carry us into winter.

III

Love, the Ugly

Our mother's hair
fell sharp
as razor wire.
Her hands morphed
to talons,
her smell,
wet iron,
and for a while,
every touch
she gave
was a cut
on us, every kiss
sent toxins
into our veins.
We could hear
how her bones
snapped, see smoke
exit at each
of their breakings,
and all through
the night
we heard
her screams,
every story
told a curse,
making
each of us
its container.

The Mound of Dust

Nothing we tried could rid us of the mound
of dust in our front yard. After us boys
had been put to bed, we heard Mom mosey
from the laundry room out the storm door
with a broom. Us boys crept from our beds
to the window watching her. Down the driveway
she floated to the mound to sweep. Endlessly,
the mound carted off down the road
in black billows more savage than smoke.
We tried to warn the neighbors, breaking through
their locked windows to watch them choke
ignoring us. We tried talking to Mom,
no hope. She continued brushing the dust.
The news reported evil among us,
but nobody knew where from, what for.
The dust rose and swirled into a screen,
blocking out the sun. Everyone was dead
or running, but none to find us
crawled back into bed, wondering
what might make Mom come back in.

Renovations

We didn't understand why she wanted them. The house long crumbled at its foundation, but on top of it, for her, we kept building. Outside, the dust stretched thickly across the sun, dimming it pale brown, making beautiful darkness of everything it shone on. We built bedrooms, parlors, and cellars with furnishings, and yet the dark stretched thicker throughout the rooms. We stopped wandering the holes of our creations and stuck together. We knew we'd lose each other like we lost our Mom if we didn't. We kept building toward the list she left, thinking she'd come out to see it all, eventually. Dad put us out to sand the staircase he built. So far into the sky it spread, so cold and breathless we became as we ascended. Our hands closed claws around the poles, up and down they went, smoothing them, while our bodies transformed under the elements. At our heights, the stairs wavered and bent. By the time we knew we'd fall, our skin speckled black and luminous, our blood thickened, and between the bones in our backs, an outward extension spread two flaps of skin so sensitive to the wind, and even knowing our mutations could carry us wherever we wanted, we merely drifted back to the ground again.

Pustule

We started to wonder how big it would grow.
Mateo's pustule started harmless,
a pinpoint. He went to sleep that night and found
a fourth of his neck under it when he woke.

He got upset. Mom told him she'd pop it,
better to be asleep than anticipate with eyes
closed, she said. It looked alien, a whole being
cocooned inside a whole planet.

The next night, it ruptures. Pus leaks
on his pillow and down the sides of his bed
in a puddle, halfway down the street.
It compelled us, even

as the pustule repaired and filled
slightly darker, a little blood at the tip.
We watched Mom heat a pin till black
at the end, then strip it with a swab.

Her dig into Mateo was thorough. She drained
his green-over-essence into a cup, snuck a bit of it
into some orange juice for his good luck
and into him from the glass it went.

Invincibility

Dad left his coffee on the counter.
It was the only thing he ever did
to make us feel invincible.

Each of us put our dusty mitts on the rim,
where we knew he wouldn't want them.
He'd never drink behind us, always let us

drink the white slivers of backwash
behind him. He'd hand us the cup or can
and tell us to run off with it, not to give it back.

That morning there were five of us
up and unwashed. Each of our mouths
on his porcelain mug for a sip.

It was forbidden. We loved it. We were sure
he wouldn't know. We left that mug steaming,
the swirled cloud brown liquid at a level

we couldn't tell apart from where it was before us.
Dad turned the corner in his uniform for work
and we scattered so fast around the house

we ended in the same incriminating spot we started.
Dad's look down at us was menacing.
We just wanted something sweet, we told him.

Impressed to Follow

Even at beatings, we'd line up
like little ducks. Resigned. Mindless.
He's going to hit us now. Stay quiet.
It'll go faster. He'll give up. Then
we can do something else. We'd take
our spreading bruises and scabs outside
and try to make nothing from them.
We'd eat TV dinners off blue cardboard
boxes when the sun went down.
Pizza. Chicken fingers. Battered.
I don't think one of us remembers
when it got sad. We think maybe
someone must've told us
because we never thought
about it. Did we need a reason
we couldn't give? We followed
our dad everywhere.

Falling Out Our Father's Mouth

Of course it's in part a good thing.
Everything inside it is a weapon.
It's hot. Cramped. We sit
in its open sores and look outward.
At night, his mouth eats, it talks
and leaves us out of it, hangs open
for the salted rims of glasses,
their liquid contents, the pull and sigh
of smoke. His tongue strains, meeting
the pink point of foreign tongues
as if in a blind slither to nowhere
while us boys dodge them both.
In the corner, we listen to the smacking
of lips, watch both junctures peel,
part, and join again on the bed,
mouth wide open to the ceiling
before folds of brown and pink
flesh eclipse us. We hold on tightly
as everything unsteadies. The stars
in the sky shrink, planets shift,
and this cave we've entered in
after him starts to sour again.
Those vapors he takes in over us.
We've come so far for our father,
but where are we? The only name
spoken is his own.

Barging In

Dad barged in after disappearing at the beginning
of the weekend. He was hungry. Mom kicked
us boys out into the daylight. She didn't give
us a timeline on when we'd be let back in,
but we'd know. My brothers and I sat in the grass,
searching those low blades
for critters to pop open.
We made a tally with three categories:
red, green, and other bloods.
The smaller ones we'd grab
between our fingers and smear
on a sheet of paper.
The bigger ones would bleed like everything else,
so as long as the blood was in good contrast
from their skin, we wouldn't need to smear them.
Me and brother Bernie wanted to line the bodies
in a row, but knowing from TV
the message that sends, Brother
used his tail to throw them off into the woods.
Our brother Mateo had wandered off and come back
with a rash. We knew we'd all be beaten
for going in dirty, but we'd get double now
one of us was hurt. When the arguments
inside turned to crashing dishes and curses,
we took to the trampoline to wail
like wild animals and distract the neighbors. We knew
all was done when things went silent. The door would
unlock and we would be let in, this time
dealing with Mateo crying rotten
to find his juice cup broken.

Folded Flesh

Our dad arranges us
into ornaments and other
furnishings throughout
an empty living room.

One by one we become
a lamp, a couch,
an entertainment center

bound so tight
in human leather
we can't get out,
and he leaves us,

creased, eventually
standing straight
but walking funny
when we're not folding
naturally in shock
to sleep.

An Occasion of Potted Meat

In all of the kitchen cabinets sits
blue-silver cans of Vienna sausages.
We can't wait to pop their tins, drain
the liquid from the round of them, six
standing in a circle at the rim of the can,
one key-locked in the center. They're soft
enough to mash to bits with the smallest
squeeze of our eager then juicy fingers.
During the course of our eating we find
pieces of meat migrating to the corners
of our lips, the tops of our tongues,
and the traps of our cheeks, and while
they dwell inside every natural crease
of our churning jaws we're happy to be
in conversation with each other as a family
of lunch eaters, laughing and smiling,
meat falling from our words to our shirts
and pants. Our belching forms a cloud
full of particle potted meat plus a sweetness
from the fruit juice we're drinking. It spreads
throughout the room of our dining to the next
room before dissipating completely. We venture
to the restroom, returning assured of our ability
to eat the remainder of the too-much-share
of meat. Using mouthwash to rinse afterward,
we spit out and downward to the sink, a wash
of rinse specked with mashed meat. Ask
any one of us now as men afraid of nitrates
the pride we had gathered around each other,
satiating, working toward finding ourselves
satiated, gestures cheap and hard won, gestures
we remember so they won't just be gone.

Mateo's Death

We haven't invited him to play. We can't stop him.
The day starts just us boys curled in front of the television,
controllers in our hands to play video games until Dad comes in.
We don't understand what makes him
so competitive with us, his children.

Mateo winning, Dad takes the controllers from the rest of us,
wanting to go head to head with the best. Mateo bests him.
Over and over Dad's blood spills in red pixels.
It seems he feels the stabs of the sword,
the singe of magic fire on his face.

While we can see that the game still plays, we also see
Dad stops playing. He grabs Mateo at the neck,
places half of his head in the carpet, the other half under his foot.
We can see Mateo pinned, his hand palm down.

We watch. Again, the line drawn is sacred. We know
we'd be damned to cross it. We look into Mateo's eyes
to remind him not to cry, watch him instead give his pained laugh.
Dad holds his head so long down there that it splits.

Something breaks in all of us as his head caves in,
more seeing it crack as an egg afterward.
Out that space comes six spiders, one with green eyes,
one canary, and a moth with blue blood on its wing.

The Thawing Season

There are times when the door to Mom's bedroom
doesn't open. Sometimes, it lasts for months.
Frost creeps from the floor tiles to the walls,
but her door still burns like a furnace. What's left
of the heat throughout the rest of the house floats
to the top. Dad shows in his red pickup. In the back
are meat hooks and long lays of chicken and beef and pork.
Through the door, Dad animates in black boots,
an apron, and rubber gloves. Before long, his frozen cast
of meats hangs above us. He puts a pot of water to boil
on the stove and looks after us. Perhaps he's lonely.
As the door to Mom's room cracks, the meat starts
to thaw. Flies gather. The hooks and meat sway
in the air above us and drip, and soften shape,
and sometimes fall on us from the ceiling.
We're covered in blood, dead meats and their juices
with our dad, and we settle in well to this routine
by the time the water boils, he's gone again.

Early That Morning Mom Rallies Her Troupe

In a line, she calls us up, dunks us for a scrub
below sudsy water then dries her boys into new men.
She gives each of us a comb over,
softens the Q-tips between her lips
before the insert and dresses us
in our best shoes and shirts.
Today we're only off to buy furniture,
but it suits our low tolerance for adventure.
On the drive, we hang our heads out the windows.
Bugs slap harder across our faces
than they ever would walking. Arrived,
we let loose in the darkly lighted warehouse.
The beds, couches, and other furnishings
are much nicer than we've ever known.
We sit and jump and sleep like adults.
We play with the store's props: wax spills
of wine and condiments like the candles
we burned ourselves with in the closet
convinced we could do magic.

The Last Time We Saw Our Dad's Face

He sat locked out of the house in the driveway.
We watched from the curtain, thinking
how we'd never sat on his chest,
never twirled our fingers through his hair,

were never close enough to know the scent
of his aftershave, despite his clean and sunken face.
There was something about the wash of the floodlights
over him. His eyes glowed golden, lighter than we knew

them, his pupils cut sharp like a cat's. I remembered
this one night walking through the house to get water,
the air wet, smelling of salt and iron. Turning the corner
into the kitchen, I found him curled dark by the light of a lamp

like some six-foot slug, had only known him there
by the click of the light and him suddenly under it,
all those freed shadows digging into him when he saw me
and said nothing. I was afraid to walk past, fearing he'd grab me,

do something to make me any more scared
and run back to my room parched. I couldn't help but think
if I started running, this might be the only time he'd

chase after me. I would make it to the room
before he did. It would be the one time I could be scared
he might break in, his strong arms leaning over, all those
moldy shadows dangling toward me from him, with the world
being then too small for me to do anything but take them in.

To the Sons

When your dad starts following you into mirrors,
you'll try to ignore him. To full resolution he'll creep
an outfit of the whole skin you wear,

and from where within you'll breathe over the years.
Underneath, you'll reach for slight evidence
that you're alive and separate.

Outside the mirrors, you'll notice.
When your body swells, it will swell like his,
and when it wilts, it will wilt like his,

and when it sags, and when it's sick.
You'll think how sound it would've been
having it all prefaced, saving days

trying to picture how you'll both perish.
Try not to take badly when somebody tells you
how you look. Nice. Like him. There will be a world

of people doing it. Try your best
to say thank you, to give something back.
Don't expect them to understand.

When you lie in bed, it's him
you'll go to sleep with. When you eat,
it's his lip that will curl around the food,

though it will be your body he nourishes.
Try to dodge mentioning how when you smear
your hands across your face to wash it,

you imagine the spread of your features as his,
that when you've blotted out all the mirrors,
even the darkness you inherit is his.

IV

Hurts Themselves

Bernie used to hurt himself. Beatings
did nothing for him, unlike the rest of us.
The tears he shed dug trails into his skin
and anything else they fell to. We told
him to be silent so he wouldn't die,
and into the cold dark of the wall he sat.
It seemed to calm him. He didn't come
when we called him from it. The dark
under and behind him would wet warm
and dry again, eventually sticking
to his back, and only then did he move it
from the wall. The dark and him had fused,
so thick and long those black strands
of darkness burrowed into him. They'd begin
to lift where we'd pull at them, but we'd let go
when we saw how that, too, hurt him.
Bernie remained calm and silent
and the darkness became an overgrowth,
and to the point that his body and eyes
showed vague shapes under shadows.
One night, after the lights went out,
we lost him. He left us. We only heard
the door open.

Where It Can't Be Seen

Lionel put a tattoo of the sun on his chest,
in the cavity right above his sternum,
before anyone would've crushed it.
He soaked the washcloth in cold water
and held it on himself till he was sure
the sun would lie perfectly. He marched
into our parents' room, pulled down
his shirt at the neck and shouted,
convinced he had powers, that he hadn't
told them, that they should understand
he was just like the kids in our favorite
television shows. Mom told him
how as a baby she'd combed him over.
If he had powers, she'd have known.
Perhaps in another time, she'd have
humored him. Lionel knew his sun was
temporary, taking so many measures
to preserve it outside its telling, going out
bare skin and foot with the exception
of trousers. He stopped brushing his teeth,
so gritsy, afraid the paste would run over
to erase. The stale smell about him got thicker,
and over his sun and chest formed a crust.
He avoided water and the wash until Mom
made him, and with the wash of every day,
his pride faded. Lionel couldn't see himself
as anything by the time his sun wiped clean,
and that's how us boys learned to bury
what we believe.

Theo

He became our only sister. Maybe he took too much
to making Mom happy as a girl. Too much disappointment
to knowing that would but couldn't make her happy.
Back when Mom thought he would be her last baby,
she told him she'd always hoped her last would be a girl.
That sometimes, she thought he was her girl, just born
with the wrong parts. Still, as our brother, Theo
spoke out to us, said, "Sometimes when I gather the skin
over my pecs and pull it toward the center of my chest,
I'm convinced I have real cleavage. I could be like the girls.
In the coming years my hair could fall thick, the darkest
brown curls, or I could straighten them and be beautiful."
He already had eyelashes that bent backward. We understood.
We were sorry. We were sad. It was when Theo started talking
like this that we hid him from our dad, pitched him
as one of the girls from down the street when he'd come in
intermittently from long stretches in the open elsewhere.
It was easy making Dad believe us. It was hard seeing him
struggle to list us all in conversation, to look us straight-faced
and forget our names, call us the convenient wild things.
How insignificant it must feel to have had us when we walk
in miniature around him and he not know us, when we bunch
in Mom's bosom, the spread of all her ambitions hidden
between us.

Earl

In truth it's been years since we understood him.
There are things we could explain, however.
How he moves like a turtle in the daytime.
How he scurries like a rat at night. We recognize
he does the best he can with words and sentences,
a tone, a body language that's coarse and slow,
but his own. We leave him where he comes and goes.
We don't ignore him, don't yell a word back at him.
We know we've pushed him in the past. In a world
of sunlight and cancer, we lay his nest, dig
his burrows. In a world of noise and missteps,
we pull his shell. Every word he leaks is ours
to fail because failure comes at so much less
and faster than success, and we're so tired now.
We wear him. His body structures so strong
for a heart so feeble and carrying it, we all stiffen
at the strides we've made to crush him, let him go
under, determine if we flood him with every violence
we've kept, exchange every tenderness we've given,
could he suffer that occasion beyond the passion toward it?

The Wilting Tree

When Lionel thought he was sneaking,
I saw him venture into the woods,
a brown satchel with little scrolls
of crinkly manila paper hanging
out on his back. I'd seen him
compose his tellings furiously,
the veins in his right arm bulging
with green and purple bruising,
and in a violent tremor on his pages,
as if his heart and mind were bleeding.
He'd place the scrolls on the tree.
Its bark would crackle and split
where it pulled the scrolls inside itself.
The tree dropped its blossoms
in a shower over him and blushed
a golden glow at its roots and canopy
while he danced under it. I could never see
the writing. Only that over time, the phrases
got shorter. Five words. Four. The last held
two. The tree took it in, same as all of them,
but whatever Lionel had lost or given killed
both of them, that vermouth we pair
with shame and quietude so as to keep
how it shows on us a secret too.

Set in Sentiment

My dad's parents live in an old house. I remember as a little boy. Mom's parents are dead. The house is dark. The corners are black. Grandma and I bake cakes. She uses a recipe, and I help out. It's our favorite thing to do. My uncle lives there, too. He has a room to himself. He brushes his teeth really hard. His teeth are so clean and golden. I hear him from the bedroom. Grandma and I play. She watches me run. She sits in her chair in pain. As a kid, I understand. She is dying. I don't go back to her house for a while. Time changes. Cartwheels. Car wrecks. Then the family is a mess.

Grandma takes me to church. There's a lady there with one leg who doesn't say anything. Grandma tells me not to stare. Granddad can't hear a damn thing. I want to play. The service is so long. He promised we'd play before going. Now he's sleeping. His eyes are closed. He looks dead. He sleeps so much because he is dying. Guaranteed. Next, he'll be eating. Routine dictates. After dinner, I'll be leaving. My grandparents move so slow and toward death.

Grandma keeps her necklaces in a box on the dresser. They are shiny and I want them until I steal them. She has so many. She doesn't notice. She says they are out of style, that they will be back. She knows I like them. She gives me the necklace her mother gave her. I learn necklaces like that one aren't worth much of anything. There's something about the sentiment. The sentiment is what I lose in some classroom around the first grade. Her house burns down. All that sentiment and so fast, burning, then dead. The dying. My grandparents have been all these years. I caught them at the wrong moment. They make me anxious. They've had such a long wait.

Family Mentality

You think of the sun as a boil,
and the clouds, gray sediment
that infects it. The light swells
with pus and dims. The sky
lets loose its infection. It falls
in drops on the house. The view
from the windows runs yellow
with steam. You think the greenery
running over the hill a mold over
everything and still reaching.
Every sound outside is a dying,
worming its way in. Beyond the hill,
where the sea lies, you've seen monsters
in crude shadows under its surface,
where you've thought to escape.
The wash of its currents an acid burn
on the sand, what remains of the Earth.
You've spent years in a state
of hardly breathing. The song you sing
for comfort plagues your mother,
makes her ruptured ears bleed
though you love her, and with nowhere
to go, holed from the world inside
your only refuge, you dread inevitably
your body will sour to waste inside it.
The scene outside and the one within
makes you question which is better.
You think to open the door like so many
before you. You've long thought the sun
at the center. Its bulging, a poison.
With a blade in hand, you stretch
your arm out for its release, as its heat
makes ash of your striving. You wave it
hoping to make your way. You wave it
hoping to make the cut that saves.

Dues

Aunt Reatha likes movies where the men die at the end, a bat to the head, blood shed after a long fall down to a death on a sharp object. She confides. I want her to be safe sharing these things with me. She smokes cigarettes in her chair and we watch the movies together after she's fed me. She makes the same thing special for every day, a hotdog with melted cheese and no bun cut to many dangling pieces. I eat. I look up to her hard face and say, "Not me, Auntie."

I'm as happy as any child left home to be raised by the moldy middle-aged nanny. I think one day, I'll have stayed over too long. My auntie rolls her hair tightly at night with plans to go out but keeps her cap and gown on the whole day inside our brick house. The smoke that cloaks her has a sweetness.

I'm not fed well here with my Auntie. She knows it. "I've lived this long," she says. "And you're just a growing boy." After my coney, I get a small treat, a plum, a slice of cake. She says she loves me. She wouldn't bait. The TV fills the room with light through the darkest. She doesn't confine me to the living room. Sometimes I play outside. I find her right where I left her when I come in and sit down. "See there," she says to me. "A good man for then. A good man for now." Her body sinks into the recliner and I stay. I take notes until I shut down. She sees me there expecting no more than her boy. Her boy walking through the door after so many years in front of the small screen watching the men pay their dues. I'm off the hook. She'll never see me that way. I'll never have to walk in and say "Auntie, me too."

Diamond Dog

Our dog has a diamond face.
He's a sweet, big-bodied dog.
A sturdy dog,
that loves us harder than any.

He's a good boy. We thank God
he's never gone missing,
that we've never struggled
for money, that we've always
had enough to eat.

We thank God for every carat
we haven't counted on that face,
for when he licks
and reminds us.

We thank God one of us
will outlive him, that when
the flesh rots off his back
and leaves us his bones,
we'll still remember that face
and where we buried it,
out back, with the rest of him.

Stressful Fits

We were afraid
to talk about them.
We thought nature
might calm Lionel.
We would let him
run out in the middle
of the yard. He'd buckle
into himself, hands
on his temples, blood
in a heavy trickle
down his nose.
The sky would darken.
The wind would stir
into a gale. The leaves
would detach
from their stems
and swirl around him.
We started putting him
in a room by himself.
The longer he wailed,
the harder the wind
crashed against
the house. Birds blew
off course, dead
before touching
the ground.
We'd find them
fallen in a black ring
around us. We thought
we could make Lionel happy
forever if we just tried

hard enough. It was
our longest aspiration,
and the saddest thing
we did. Then we thought
he might kill us,
which taught us
how quickly intention
flees the will to live.

Our Sister Theo

Theo grew his hair down to his ankles. He'd have ground
his jaw down smooth if he could. Where his arms and legs
were hard, he'd lather cream to soften and make them
glisten. Where his body swung at sharp angles, he'd make
arcs to round them, and where his voice fell low, he raised it,
but never to the kind of high he needed. His body
only changed short of the thing it was becoming.
When is it that for another, one becomes willing to change
everything? And what of the former left sitting dark
in that cold damp cellar, in that puddle of still water,
dirt grown up its skin, stuck to the wall by shackles
around its ankles with the swipe of waste around its mouth to taint
what small nutrient was last given to it? What of how it cranes
its head to stare as if to ask how exactly has it been made
to feel sorry? And why?

v

Spectacle

Our aunt only has one boob. It's really big.
There are three nubs where we guess the other
one was. We don't know. Something happened
to it. She wears the four of them proudly
under clothing. Whatever questions there are,
we don't ask. There's this kid Wesley
in our neighborhood who asks a lot of questions.
His mother makes great cake. We take advantage
and think nothing of it. Our aunt has given
us permission. In the mornings, she props herself
in the window to read the paper. Light streams in
on her housecoat and for a moment everything
about her shines. We lead Wesley along outside,
just shy her peripheral visions, to stare at her.
We get cake. No one tells us our attractions
are morbid. Our aunt tells us everything
about our family is something to stare at,
but it's rare that we turn a profit. Most kids
still call boobs balls at our age, three-foot-tall
people with requests for girls with big balls,
as if. They don't know like we do when
they're as big as our aunt's that's not at all
how they fall, that nothing falls as it stands
or once did and it takes a bit of learning
to walk away with something more than sadness.
We've often thought later, after we've misplaced
all our early embarrassment, how to supplement
everything that's gone missing, picturing
our aunt pulling from the one boob she's got
to inflate the other, so she wouldn't have to
walk around and be patient, so she could loosen
some of the pride she's held on to that all
she's left with on the other side are pieces.

Sleeping with Grandfather

I remember Mom threading the needle,
lashing the stitch back and forth in her hands.
Grandfather had just died. We found him dead
on the hardwood, skin still vibrant and moist.
No time to waste, Mom peeled him in long, shapely strips,
then cut them into worthy squares. Grandfather
would become a blanket, an otherwise mixed message
for us to sleep under. Mom paid a guy
$50 to dig a hole to throw him in, and another twenty
to cover it up. She sat around the plot making the quilt,
and we sat a skirt around her while she told the story of him.
Bastard, always made off on cold nights, paying for warmth
he hadn't bothered to find right in front of him, but I promise,
she said, you all will have. He won't take that away from you,
and it'll kill him, you know, shacking up to benefit his own kin.
And she was right. All those years, we had him.
At bedtime, we'd pull him back from the headboard,
tucking ourselves feet first before pulling him over our faces.

Autobiography

I was taken in by two wolves whose whole diet was bacon.
Each morning we shared the nine packs of bacon we fried then ran.
We ran so fast the woods stretched a band of evergreen.

We ran faster than life. We watched the nine-year-old flower girls
in the forest live out their whole lives. Each morning they lived
and before the end of our daily run in the afternoon they died again.

Their hair curled brown to fall flat-white, their skin opaque
before filling with light. Never mind the things they did.
I named my favorite Heather. Her life and death,

mere markers on the trail. We ran so fast the fat in our arteries
would expand then explode and collapse, spilling out and over
like liquid cheese. It smelled like bacon, bacon all fat and no lean:

a treat. Our hearts came up our throats and out our mouths so tasty
and we kept running. We were together and happy. We had everything
and we could keep it. We ran past our own deaths, and when we came
up on our hearts again we picked them up and swallowed them.

Family Festers

Our brother has a girlfriend. He doesn't like us anymore.
He doesn't like his girlfriend, either. We only tell people
that she's pretty, but we don't always remember.
We imagine them holding hands in the street, going
into dark places with couple's lighting, insisting on sitting
side by side with dreams they don't wake up to of sitting
elsewhere. We get to see them on holidays. They gather
at Mom's cooking like flies we don't swat after.
At the dinner table, we're the only ones that talk to his girl.
We wonder a lot about the arrangements they've made,
why they don't speak to each other every moment
they're sitting mouths closed and not eating, but it suits us.
We make discoveries and think little of our brother
and the escape he made but can't maintain in his off-season
of mating. He's done this before, trailed off to another girl
and come back with her, come back just himself without her,
warped and moving around so slowly. We feed him
until he's well enough to leave again. We don't say this to him
because he remembers, but we'll always be his.

In Families

Sometimes the truth is used to fill space. It's recreation,
four beers into the patio barbecue, when everyone sits
at a slant in their chairs and makes finger food of the entrees
they'd otherwise put neatly on paper plates. There's no telling
exactly how it starts, where it comes from. Looking around
at the stars' crystal twinkling, the tarp of the night's sky,
toes peeking through sandals, tossed shoes and socks
next to bare feet on wood, there's a haze about everyone,
an otherworldly feel in part thanks to the torches' dancing
flames shifting shadows on everyone's faces, sending them
into their mood, the one that knows there's no need
to hurt anyone, but says let's do anyway, the one
that locks Auntie in the bathroom, sends Uncle down
with bruises and a broken tooth, cuts Mom loose, sends
Dad off, everything to lose, and us young ones to clean
everything up, to find the right words to say now that the truth
is unbound again, breaking through everything with a charge
from its gates.

Family Feuds

I can't brush them away.
Like most things, I do
what's necessary to win.
It's so important.
And sometimes I'm cruel.
The words stream
from my mouth
as if no lips are in place
to hold them,
as if that opening
is all gape and teeth,
but every now and then,
when I'm still active
in the argument,
something reminds me
of all the things
I hate most about me.
How is it again I find
me attacking me
attacking them?
Another onslaught
in all directions,
its familiar origin.
I'm frightened,
but it doesn't stop me.
For years I was
at the losing end
of these fights,
my family all there to see.
Now I tell myself I'm the best
at hurting people. I'm willing.
I'm trying to be. I think
there's something I want.
I want this argument
to tell me before it ends.

Our Father's New Body

Lays of skin trailed behind its slow movement: dark, gray-wrinkly strips
with hard hair like an elephant's. They hit the ground in splashes,
as if in a dive to someplace important, but they just squirmed
on the ground where they curled dehydrated, their undersides
red-pink with the smell of decay. We went behind them,
collecting the pieces in ice-water as though we could save them.
Between our Dad's thin words and departures, we were unsure
of where exactly inside the body we could reach in and find him.
It helped to look in his eyes, raw need inside them
but still without welcome or gratitude. What skin remained
hung long on him and away from his doings. At night,
when he turned over scared from the dreams that chased him,
his skin poured from the bed to the floor like vomit.
In the mornings, he'd go in on the toilet. No one saw him until noon.
We'd send one of us in to clean after him, but it was always as if he never went.
Despite it, we still fed him, knowing there are things no son can get away with,
even as our Dad's body separated in our hands as we bathed it.
The pull of his crevices with raised masses underneath. Us boys look back
and agree we must've helped him that little-huge bit that was possible.
In the last of it, the skin pulled so sharply against his jaw we swore with it
we could cut mountains. Maybe at a certain point we always knew
we could remove him, but we wouldn't, less whatever sadness
it would've been so easy, our Dad so little in his body and the world
as to slip with one grudge into the next.

Hardest Dying

Inside Earl's body are blooms.
We picture them beautiful.
Robust. Exotic colors. Perhaps

everyone else just thinks he's fat,
the deposits taking strange,
bulky forms and in clumps,

in pockets instead of an even spread,
a bulge we could call a belly.
He takes our father's dying

the hardest. He's mad at him
like none of us can understand.
Every day Earl gets up, runs

six miles to the lake, enough tears
in his eyes and down his face
to raise the water by inches. We worry

Earl would just raise Dad again
from any six feet under we'd bury him.
All that tension and anticipating

we watch but can't help. We don't
know if it's Dad's death he wants
or if that would make it worse. The state

of being they're both in, so turbulent.
Everyone gets shaky. Nobody gets
any rest around here, and Earl, his body

gets so heavy and every day, every run
to the water, he carries it that way,
and we every other way. We've learned

to live like this. It's not like this we hope
to stay. For change we're prepared to lose
them both, but for both of them, we'll wait.

Night-groomed

Fog looms in the dark, over the field,
the blank stare of deer. All those legs
and hooves, some to be turned upright,
crisscrossed and broken by morning.

Nights like these cold seeps into us boys' dreams,
works the phlegm in our chests into an itch-charged rattle
on our lungs and gives intention to our breathing.
Tonight, below the headboard of our beds,

we'll transform under battered consciousness,
sprout two legs and on four sprawl out in all directions,
fixed and separate and chosen, and, like the deer,
our feet will chomp through and pierce, break white

on white ice and snow down to its brown dirt bone.
Free roaming, we'll prance about,
let our nature fall from and out our bodies.
This night and every other we dream

we've always been reaching higher
than our arms could raise us, higher than
our caregivers could lift. These dreams
do better than we could pretend, protect us

from the reality. And though we've seen
how it all could end, at least then, when
our eyes open, we'll wake up bundled
beside each other, all-warm and tucked
in.

The Dreamed Destination

I dreamt I was on a boat sailing
over an ocean I didn't know. No crew
on board to navigate, help row,
just the whip of the sail in the wind,
the brood of thunder, its lighting kin,
and the sheeted pelt of rain; carried
by the sea's other elements, filtered
through a dark lens. I stood leaning
over the port, staring into the water,
listening to its drone-like roaring,
glimpsing the textures of its unrest
between its splashes over me. I dreamt
as a child, screaming toward the cut
of the bow, feeling the sound curl
a backward trajectory from the one
I traveled without light, aimlessly.
In the distance were bush fires and men
dancing around them on a coast separated
in shades from the ocean by its darkness
and homemade illumination. I felt
I was approaching home but dreading it.
Plowing head first, I watched the ship
break, sink down a depth I wouldn't dare
traverse again. Toward the fires I walked
familiar, grains of sand beneath my feet.
The men on the beach were cooking over a spit,
each of them wore my siblings on their faces.
I ran to them, holding out my forearm in greeting.
The flesh they peeled from it to eat stripped me
down to the white meat, but returned with each
eaten piece. Sick as I felt, chunk by chunk
the skin recovered my arm's veins and vessels,
the rush of blood returning color as I stood.

The Afterthought

From my hotel room, there's a clear view of the ocean.
I'm high enough to be eye level with the lease
of the water and the sky. With no sand in sight,

I'm anticipating an end. I'm in a bad mood,
but on the balcony, it's an afterthought, occurring
like puberty and everything else gradual and evident

post process. I take myself seriously. I imagine
a rock the size of a world falling through
the gray and blue hues, into greater perspective

as it drives away the surrounding water.
I think about my family
because that's what people tell you

you're supposed to do when you find yourself at an end.
They're in the next room. They've already pissed me off.
I think I should warn them that this is coming,

but it's not foreboding like the promise of a private reprimand.
It's beautiful. I can feel gusts of wind on my face.
I can see waves, the atmosphere clearing the way,

making the spectacle available to the stars.
It's as if the rock is wrapped around something
central in myself. I can feel everything I've held back

wallow in my throat. The feeling purges further up
my neck and gropes all those locked tears behind my eyes,
but I keep them. I need to see this clearly.

The rock draws farther down and seems to bob
like a ball, a toy boat, not quite sinking.
Then it does. There's a flash of light, a shockwave,

bright and warm as I close my eyes and take
the last air. I can't take that magic
with me to dinner, but I go anyway.

The appetizer, main course, and dessert
leave me empty, and all I can think
until the next time it happens is that I've lost it.

ACKNOWLEDGMENTS

Boundless thanks to Cynthia Hogue, Norman Dubie, Sally Ball, James Kimbrell, John Gosslee, Andrew Sullivan, and everyone at C&R Press.

Warm thanks to Jillian Weise, Glenn Shaheen, Josh Bell, Brandon Rushton, Paige Lewis, Brionne Janae, Caroline Randall Williams, Cam Awkward-Rich, Tonya Wiley, Taylor Johnson, Matthew Broaddus, Crystal Boson, Quincy Scott Jones, Andriniki Mattis, Yolanda Franklin, Cave Canem, Tanya Grae, Eleanor Mary Boudreau, Will Fargason, Jessie King, Marianne Chan, Brandi Nicole Martin, Dorsey Olbrich, and Aram Mrjoian.

Sincere thanks to the editorial staffs of the publications in which these poems first appeared:

"Paternity" in *TriQuarterly*
"The Last Time We Saw Our Dad's Face" and "Our Father's New Body" in *Saranac Review*
"Sleeping with Grandfather," "The Thawing Season," "Theo," and "Our Sister Theo" in *Origins Literary Journal*
"Family Mentality," "Dues," and "Autobiography" in *The Spectacle*
"A Subtext for Violence" and "Folding Flesh" in *decomP*
"A Palace of Ice" and "Love, the Ugly" in *Connotation Press: An Online Artifact*
"Falling Out Our Father's Mouth" in *Vinyl Poetry*
"The Flame in Mother's Mouth," "Set in Sentiment," and "Diamond Dog" in *Public Pool*
"To the Sons" in *Bennington Review*

C&R PRESS TITLES

NONFICTION

Women in the Literary Landscape by Doris Weatherford, et al
Credo: An Anthology of Manifestos & Sourcebook for Creative
Writing by Rita Banerjee and Diana Norma Szokolyai

FICTION

Last Tower to Heaven by Jacob Paul
No Good, Very Bad Asian by Lelund Cheuk
Surrendering Appomattox by Jacob M. Appel
Made by Mary by Laura Catherine Brown
Ivy vs. Dogg by Brian Leung
While You Were Gone by Sybil Baker
Cloud Diary by Steve Mitchell
Spectrum by Martin Ott
That Man in Our Lives by Xu Xi

SHORT FICTION

Notes From the Mother Tongue by An Tran
The Protester Has Been Released by Janet Sarbanes

ESSAY AND CREATIVE NONFICTION

In the Room of Persistent Sorry by Kristina Marie Darling
The internet is for real by Chris Campanioni
Immigration Essays by Sybil Baker
Je suis l'autre: Essays and Interrogations
by Kristina Marie Darling
Death of Art by Chris Campanioni

POETRY

A Family Is a House by Dustin Pearson
The Miracles by Amy Lemmon
Banjo's Inside Coyote by Kelli Allen
Objects in Motion by Jonathan Katz
My Stunt Double by Travis Denton
Lessons in Camoflauge by Martin Ott
Millennial Roost by Dustin Pearson
Dark Horse by Kristina Marie Darling
All My Heroes are Broke by Ariel Francisco
Holdfast by Christian Anton Gerard
Ex Domestica by E.G. Cunningham
Like Lesser Gods by Bruce McEver
Notes from the Negro Side of the Moon by Earl Braggs
Imagine Not Drowning by Kelli Allen
Notes to the Beloved by Michelle Bitting
Free Boat: Collected Lies and Love Poems by John Reed
Les Fauves by Barbara Crooker
Tall as You are Tall Between Them by Annie Christain
The Couple Who Fell to Earth by Michelle Bitting
Notes to the Beloved by Michelle Bitting

CPSIA information can be obtained
at www.ICGtesting.com
Printed in the USA
FSHW010851180319
56389FS